Tell Me the Stories of Jesus

Art by **Del Parson** • Lyrics by **William H. Parker**

Art © 2019 Del Parson
For more information about art prints by Del Parson,
please visit www.havenlight.com or call 1-800-366-2781

ISBN: 978-0-9984244-5-3

Published by HavenLight
American Fork, UT 84003
www.HavenLight.com

HAVENLIGHT
FINE ART PUBLISHING

Tell Me the Stories of Jesus

Art by **Del Parson** • Lyrics by **William H. Parker**

Tell me the stories of Jesus
I love to hear

Things I would ask him
to tell me
If he were here

Scenes by the wayside tales of the sea

Stories of Jesus
tell them to me.

First let me hear how the children stood round his knee

And I shall fancy his blessings resting on me

Words full of kindness deeds full of grace

All in the love-light
of Jesus' face.

Tell me in accents of wonder
how rolls the sea

Tossing the boat in a tempest on Galilee

And how the Master
ready and kind

Chided the billows
and hushed the wind.